STATESIDE

STATESIDE

poems

Jehanne Dubrow

Foreword by Ted Kooser

TRIQUARTERLY BOOKS
NORTHWESTERN UNIVERSITY PRESS
EVANSTON, ILLINOIS

TriQuarterly Books
Northwestern University Press
www.nupress.northwestern.edu

Printed in the United States of America

10   9   8   7   6   5   4   3   2

Library of Congress Cataloging-in-Publication Data

Dubrow, Jehanne.
    Stateside : poems / Jehanne Dubrow ; foreword by Ted Kooser.
       p. cm.
    ISBN 978-0-8101-5214-4 (pbk. : alk. paper)
    I. Title.
  PS3604.U276S73 2010
  811.6—dc22

                                                          2009043327

∞ The paper used in this publication meets the minimum requirements of the
American National Standard for Information Sciences—Permanence of Paper for
Printed Library Materials, ANSI Z39.48-1992.

CONTENTS

Part One

Part Two

Part Three

As I read the poems in this remarkable and moving collection, I was reminded again and again of the wool sweaters knitted by the wives of Irish fishermen. According to tradition, each sweater is made with its own unique design, a combination of knots, cables, and braids, so that if the fisherman's body should wash up along the coast, his widow can identify him.

It takes skillful hands and a good many hours to make a sweater, and the person knotting and tying the yarn must keep her eye on the task, making precise decisions as she proceeds. That's the manner in which the best poems are written, too, with consummate thought and care. And one can easily imagine what might go through a woman's mind as she works, what intimations of providence she feels as she knits beside her window opening onto the impersonal, silencing sea.

These well-crafted poems by Jehanne Dubrow are, at least for this one reader, like those beautiful and altogether necessary sweaters. They have been patiently, thoughtfully, and artfully knitted by a sometimes anguished, sometimes resigned, and always hopeful young woman, well acquainted with the perils of the sea, the perils of war, the perils of loneliness, seeing her husband's ship just a spot on the horizon, sailing away.

Of course, Dubrow recognizes the antiquity and depth of tradition of which these poems are a part and a continuance. Women have suffered these fearful absences for countless centuries. Those poems in which she identifies with Penelope attest to that. And the poet's responses to uncertainty are as various as are those of the generations of women who have waited, stateside, for their men to return.

In Ezra Pound's translation of a thousand-year-old Old English poem, "The Seafarer," an anonymous sailor says,

> *May I, for my own self, song's truth reckon,*
> *Journey's jargon, how I in harsh days*
> *Hardship endured oft.*

Well, that's the sailor's side of it, isn't it? You are about to read the other side of the hardship, in the carefully cast words of the wife left onshore.

TED KOOSER

ACKNOWLEDGMENTS

Barrow Street: "Navy Housing" and "Nonessential Equipment"

Birmingham Poetry Review: "Against War Movies," "Eastern Shore," "A Short Study of Catastrophe," and "Stateside"

caesura: "Secure for Sea"

Evansville Review: "O' Dark Hundred"

If: "Whiskey Tango Foxtrot"

Mezzo Cammin: "In Penelope's Bedroom," "Penelope Considers a New 'Do," and "Penelope, On a Diet"

MiPOesias: "Silver Spring"

New England Review: "Oenophilia"

The Pedestal: "After Visiting the USS *Anzio*"

Poetry Daily: "Sea Change"

Prairie Schooner: "Ithaca," "Penelope, Stateside," "Reading Stephen Crane's 'War Is Kind' to My Husband," "The Rooted Bed," "Sea Change," and "Surface Warfare"

Third Coast: "Bowl, in the Shape of a Bristol Boat"

Umbrella: "At the Mall with Telemachus," "Odysseus, Sleeping," and "Penelope, Pluperfect"

War, Literature and the Arts: "Argos"

Women's Review of Books: "On the Erotics of Deployment" and "Shabbat Prayer, on the Occasion of War"

"VJ Day in Times Square" won a Bright Lights Big Verse award, sponsored by the Poetry Society of America and the Times Square Alliance.

◥

I am extremely grateful for the support of the Virginia Center for the Creative Arts, the Sewanee Writers' Conference, the West Chester Poetry Conference, and the University of Nebraska–Lincoln.

I also want to thank the poets, teachers, and friends who have nudged, coaxed, and cheered this book into existence: Daniel Anderson, Leslie Harrison, Andrew Hudgins, Ted Kooser, David Mason, Kristin Naca, and Hilda Raz. A special thanks to Mike Levine at Northwestern University Press.

Finally, my love and thanks to my parents, Jeannette and Stephen Dubrow, to my brother, Eric, and to my puppy, Argos. And to my husband, Jeremy, without whom there would be no *Stateside.*

STATESIDE

PART ONE

SECURE FOR SEA

maritime terminology

It means the moveable stays tied.
Lockers hold shut. The waves don't slide
a metal box across the decks,
or scatter screws like jacks, the sea
like a rebellious child that wrecks
all tools which aren't fastened tightly
or fixed.
       At home, we say *secure*
when what we mean is letting go
of him. And even if we're sure
he's coming back, it's hard to know:
the farther out a vessel drifts,
will contents stay in place, or shift?

ASSATEAGUE ISLAND, MARCH

We toss our coffee on the sand, watching
the liquid sink and fade to almost nothing
like disappearing ink. The wind disturbs
our tent flap, jostles the poles, sways the frame
so that I hope we cannot stay the night.
Why don't we leave? I ask. He shakes his head,
and in my borrowed sleeping bag I lie
awake, shiver beneath its summer weight,
curl myself into a question mark.
I listen, for hours, to the pace of waves
an irritant like sand inside a shoe.
He always shuts his eyes before I do.
He's slumped in front of the TV or pinned
by an opened book across his chest, and here
surrounded by the racket nature makes,
he rests, so deep asleep I don't exist.
At 8 A.M., we stand, roll up our beds.
I couldn't sleep at all, he says. *Too cold,*
though you seemed fine. I laugh. To think
of all those hours I listened for his breath
and he for mine, the air a frozen wing,
the wild ponies snuffling for food.
Goddamn our domesticity. At least
we should have sighed the other's name, or rubbed
together, tried burning like two broken sticks.

O' DARK HUNDRED

This is the hour that writers eulogize,
      midnights when my husband guards his post
against monotony. Before sunrise,
      this is the hour that writers eulogize.
In port, a sentry walks the deck, replies
      all conditions normal, surveys the coast.
This is the hour that writers eulogize,
      midnights when my husband guards his post.

I can imagine that he faces west,
      the sky like a purple sail above the sea.
Somewhere a buoy creeks. Waves sink or crest,
      and I imagine him. He faces west
to stand and watch and wait alone, the rest
      of the crew asleep in the machinery.
I can imagine him. He's facing west,
      the sky a purple sail above the sea.

My words are just reflections from the shore,
      and the page, imperfect mirror of his ship,
where white lights blink above each metal door.
      My words are just reflections. On the shore
there's radio silence—no talk of war,
      only the sound of nothing, only the blip
of words reflecting distantly from shore,
      and the page, imperfect mirror of his ship.

AFTER VISITING THE USS *ANZIO*

We walked the pier to see the cruiser, moored
with Kevlar lines thick as limbs, then came aboard,
where decks vibrated underneath the weight
of polished brass and perforated steel.

My husband pointed out the fire main
and cable run, explained scuttles and where
the ladders led. I don't remember much
he said, but only know he placed my hand

against a hatch to feel the engines tense,
the systems like a pulse inside my palm.
And then, the CIC, where it was calm
and quiet to the passageway—

                              In war
he'll stand before the green displays of light,
evaluate a signal's frequency.
He'll chart trajectories and blips across

a screen. And all the ship will swallow him:
its hull, an ashy paint they call *haze gray*
(*haze gray and under way,* say the sailors,
kissing their wives good-bye), a silver gray

of knives, of mist which settles on the water,
a gray so like the moon, its surface strewn
with oceans, bays, and seas that tremble with
the burden of their wide tranquility.

VIRGINIA BEACH

Tonight we're kids again, all summers boring
as peacetime, our grown-up lives distant

like the barrel organ grinding through a song,
the revolution of the Ferris wheel.

If we look far enough beyond the strand,
we'll see your cruiser there, a blurred knife

that separates the water from its skin,
quiet as modern warfare often is.

Rocky road drips chocolate on your hands.
You lick each fingertip, gesture at a ship

so that it disappears behind your palm,
the naval station still within your reach,

so near we smell the breath of diesel fuel.
I would like to call it death, this thing that sticks

like marshmallows inside my mouth, gritty
with a thousand sharp particulates of sea.

NEWPORT

You lead the puppy past the moored boat.
He nuzzles sand, runs to where the waves break,
    snaps at lacquered fish that swim near shore.
You let him off the leash, because you like
    to see the freedom of a loosened thing,
a ball releasing from a hand, a voice
    untying from the collar of the throat.
Each day you walk a little farther, then bring
    him home to me, his tail a muddy spike,
his body soggy as a kitchen mop.
    We don't wring him dry but watch him shake
the ocean out, watch him rub his face across
    the carpet until he falls asleep, sopping,
curled tightly as a seashell on the floor.

SILVER SPRING

Montgomery County, Md.

It's light above. Below,
inside the red-line metro,

the evening never sheds itself for day,
but curves into a passageway,

a universe of fang and tail.
We're lit by bulbs whose pale

fluorescent eyes shine on, unblinkingly.
The third rail sibilates with electricity.

And we—alone
—stand frozen by a sound, the drone

of trains, sidewinders sliding through
blue corridors, steel sinew

stretched to breaking,
metallic snakes,

their scales aluminum
instead of skin.

Warm-blooded creatures don't belong
so deeply underground. We aren't strong

enough to fight the rattlesnake,
the way it coils into wire, then slowly shakes

its body as it strikes.
We wait. The subway hisses like

a diamondback.
A shadow-monster slithers down the track.

LOVE IN THE TIME OF COALITION

He whispers *weapons of mass destruction*
against the sand dune of her skin. She's toxin.

She's liquid sarin. She's pure plutonium.
Her tracers burn and dim and burn again.

As last resort, he holds a congressional inquiry
about her lips. *Have you no sense of decency,*

he asks her body's gulf. She's marsh and salt,
alluvial. She's Tigris and Euphrates.

He never finds an answer for her sleep,
more sudden than shrapnel, or for her waking,

sharper than a dust storm in the desert. She's dry
instead, made empty as a wadi,

waiting for rainfall to fill her watercourse
and for the nights to carve a temporary truce.

SEA CHANGE

Imagine this: salt water scrubbing sand
        into my husband's skin,
his fingers pale anemones, his hands
            turned coral reef, and in
      his eyes the nacreous pearls of Ariel.
This could be my husband, drowning in the swell.

A sea change means a shift, a change of heart,
        and how the oceans turn
glass shards into a jewel, rip apart
           familiar things. Waves churn.
      The surf is a liquid body that peels
a carrier from bow to stern, the keel

bent back, steel bands pliable as kelp.
        And long before I wake,
the sailors drown. No point in calling help.
           Each night, my husband shakes
      me out of sleep. I cannot reach for him
or drag him to the surface so he'll swim.

WHISKEY TANGO FOXTROT

what the fuck?

Foxtrot the Navy, I yell into the phone,
the first time that my husband groans *deployed,*
a word we've waited for since war began
four years ago.
          [Let *whiskey* slide as slow
as bullets down my throat. Let *foxtrot* be
both verb and noun.]
                    Foxtrot the Navy,
I say again but softer than before,
as if the whisper of a dance could keep
him here.
        [I need a shot of *whiskey* just
to take the news, a song in 2/4 time
and rhinestone shoes.]
                  Foxtrot, I sigh—
third time's the charm in everything but war,
oh ugly, big sublime. I'm buzzing with
white noise.
        [Call in the dancing girls,
the boys who swallow slugs from jerricans,
moonshine sloshed to the brim of each canteen.
Let *whiskey* taste toxic as benzene.]

NONESSENTIAL EQUIPMENT

The dog and I are first among those things
that will not be deployed with him. Forget
civilian clothes as well. He shouldn't bring
too many photographs, which might get wet,
the faces blurred. He only needs a set
of uniforms. Even his wedding ring
gives pause (what if it fell?—he'd be upset
to dent or scratch away the gold engraving).
The seabag must be light enough to sling
across his shoulder, weigh almost nothing,
each canvas pocket emptied of regret.
The trick is packing less. No wife, no pet,
no perfumed letters dabbed with *I-love-yous*,
or anything he can't afford to lose.

SWIM TEST

In the swimming pool, my husband is a stone
that cannot float—he's made for running
through our neighborhood, which leads him down

to where the concrete goes to gravel, then turns
to harrowed fields at the edge of town,
where wind pushes through the corn,

and the crow that drags itself up sounds like a man
drowning. All things sound like drowning if you listen.
There are other guys who sink, the ones grown

up in cinder-block cities who have never seen
the beach, or the ones like my husband, too thin
for buoyancy. They have learned to inflate their own

shirts, blow bubbles of air in the sleeves, fasten
the limbs together, a raft that holds them on
the surface long enough. After a deepwater jump, then

a fifty-yard swim, the sailors lie prone.
They're flotsam drifting in the ocean.
The hardest part is playing dead, to be broken,

inert, when what the body wants is motion,
to kick like a sprinter toward the finish line,
at least to tread water, not to breathe it in.

A SHORT STUDY OF CATASTROPHE

We're arguing about his death again.
Because all men are fools, he swears

I won't be anywhere near the fighting.
I try to laugh but can't, imagining

the photographs of Humvees overturned
like dead roaches, so burned their shells curl back

to show the offal packed inside. *Guys die
just driving from the base. The fucking place*

is cursed, I say. It's hard remaining calm.
Each conversation holds a roadside bomb,

a sniper in the window, insurgents on
the ground below. Tell me. How did the Greeks

learn beauty from that sudden turn we call
catastrophe?—the king disposed with three

quick blows, the wailing child, the wife,
and always then the falling   falling knife.

AGAINST WAR MOVIES

I see my husband shooting in *Platoon*,
and there he is again in *M*A*S*H* (how weird
to hear him talk like Hawkeye Pierce), and soon
I spot him everywhere, his body smeared
with mud, his face bloodied. He's now the star
of every ship blockade and battle scene—
The Fighting 69th, A Bridge Too Far,
Three Kings, Das Boot, and *Stalag 17.*
In *Stalingrad* he's killed, and then
he's killed in *Midway* and *A Few Good Men.*
He's burned or gassed, he's shot between the eyes,
or shoots himself when he comes home again.
Each movie is a training exercise,
a scenario for how my husband dies.

BEFORE THE DEPLOYMENT

He kisses me before he goes. While I,
still dozing, half-asleep, laugh and rub my face

against the sueded surface of the sheets,
thinking it's him I touch, his skin beneath

my hands, my body curving in to meet
his body there. I never hear him leave.

But I believe he shuts the bedroom door,
as though unsure if he should change his mind,

pull off his boots, crawl beneath the blankets
left behind, his hand a heat against my breast,

our heart rates slowing into rest. Perhaps
all good-byes should whisper like a piece of silk—

and then the quick surprise of waking, alone
except for the citrus ghost of his cologne.

READING STEPHEN CRANE'S
"WAR IS KIND" TO MY HUSBAND

I packed your seabag
today: six pairs
of pants, shirts folded in
their rigid squares,

your socks balled up
like tan grenades.
I put my photo in
as well, laid

it there between
the Kevlar vest and heap
of clothes. Don't weep,
the poet warns, don't weep.

On *60 Minutes,*
a soldier turns
his face toward us, shows
the camera his burns,

small metal slivers still
embedded in
the skin, his mouth a scrap
of ragged tin.

The young man's face
was beautiful before,
smooth, unblemished as
my own. *For war*

is kind, I read. *Great is*
the battle-god
and great the auguries,
the firing squad,

the sickly green of night
vision that cuts
the darkness open at
its seams, gutted

and spilling on the sand.
Great is the Glock,
the Aegis Combat System,
the Blackhawk

circling. Great are the Ka-Bar
fighting knives,
the shells that sing through air,
as though alive.

PART TWO

THE ROOTED BED

One moment he seemed . . . Odysseus to the life—
the next, no, he was not the man she knew.

—*THE ODYSSEY,* BOOK 23

I'm stateside now, my husband six months gone.
   I think of another soldier and his wife—
they built their bedpost from an olive tree,
   roots spreading underfoot, gray branches splayed
like fingers, floorboards grassy as a lawn.
   The tree grew through the center of their life.
They slept beneath its living canopy.
   And once the wife was left alone, its shade
stroked darkened hands across her brow.
   I like to imagine that she often thought
of chopping down the trunk, fed up with boughs
   which dropped their leaves, black fruit turning to rot.
I can't help asking if, when he came home,
   did they lie together there or sleep alone?

ARGOS

While my husband is deployed, I name
   our puppy for the dog who recognized
     Odysseus, knew him despite disguise,
  the king dressed as a beggar but still the same

familiar scent of metal on his skin,
   that same swagger beneath the cloak of rags,
     that sinewed voice. Argos, a fleabag,
  a sack of mange, nothing but skeleton.

What kind of instinct is such loyalty?
   Bred in the bone, certain as the sound
     of waves. No wonder that the wolfhound
  barked at the beach for twenty years, the sea

remaining empty, a tarnished piece of steel.
   No wonder that he learned to sight each ship
     along the sleek horizon, yipping
  at vessels that docked, nipping the heels

of every man in Ithaca. It must
   have hurt, as though from an old wound, to wait
     those twenty years beside the palace gate.
  Each night he watched the sky fade into rust.

Like a thirst so deep it hollowed out the throat,
   like a craving for salt air—he must have known
     that it's a body's faithfulness alone
  which made him keep his vigil for the boat.

ITHACA

There's war beyond the shores. But here
    there's Dairy Queen and Taco Bell,
        the Westfield Shopping Mall, the cell
            phone superstore, Home Depot, Sears.

And home remains a metaphor
    for something else: a wife who tries
        to guard her chastity, ties
            it like a yellow ribbon to her door,

sticks it to the bumper of
    her car, so that the neighbors know
        she sleeps alone, almost a widow
            to the Trojan War, her love

preserved in plastic wrap like some
    dessert too beautiful to taste.
        At PTA meetings, she's chased
            by divorcés and other glum

suitors. Nobody seems to care
    that she still wears a wedding ring.
        Odysseus is gone—same thing
            as being dead. And so men stare

at her when she buys groceries
    or takes the dog out for a pee.
        She's Ithaca, trapped in her own body,
            an island circled by the seas.

PENELOPE, STATESIDE

On an island called America,
    start fantasizing of the sex
        you had with him. Go shop for bras
           and lacy thongs at the PX,

black garters, bustiers, a cream
    that leaves your body woven silk,
        a self-help book for self-esteem,
           a bag of M&Ms, skim milk

to keep you thin, and Lean Cuisine
    (you hate to cook for one). Or buy
        a pair of True Religion jeans,
           the denim pressing on each thigh

so that there's no sensation but
    blue fabric like a second skin,
        no lover's touch more intimate
           than the zipper pressing in.

But don't forget. He may come home
    so torn that purchases won't mean
        a thing, not the Posturepedic foam
           pillowtop mattress, or the sateen

duvet. He won't be satisfied—
    by eiderdowns or bedspreads sewn
        by hand—still numb, because he's stateside
           and dreaming of the combat zone.

PENELOPE, ON A DIET

She's tried them all before
   and always failed, the war
      against her waistline more

than she can win alone,
   eating dinner on her own:
      some broth, a chicken bone

clad in a scrap of meat,
   a lettuce leaf replete
      with vinegar. Defeat

is just a Hershey's bar
   away, the gallon jar
      of peanut butter not far

enough beyond her reach.
   Some dieters beseech
      the gods for help. South Beach

and Atkins are divine,
   two deities thin as twine.
      Some women choose to dine

on nothing but the breeze,
   or no white foods, or string cheese,
      ham, and raspberries.

Some women pick protein
   instead of carbs, caffeine
      instead of lunch. They've seen

the opposite of fat
    is never thin—it's that
        solitude she can't combat,

no matter what she eats.
    She's still alone, still cheating
        on a fast she won't complete.

Another diet. There will
    be no way then to fill
        her stomach up, no pill

to kill the appetite.
    Alone, she will recite
        a prayer for each bite

of food. How good to digest
    cardboard, how very blessed
        that thirst can be suppressed.

AT THE MALL WITH TELEMACHUS

First, he's pouting for
      French fries, a chocolate shake,
a toy from Burger King,
      and what a big mistake
if she doesn't give in—
      a fit of temper in
the food court, his legs a blur
      of speed, ten out of ten
on the tantrum scale,
      his voice an ambulance
at siren pitch, my god,
      the screaming, the stridence
of his lungs, how long he holds
      each note, melismatic
as a mystic in a trance,
      or how his body's frantic
with its tick-tick-ticking,
      a toddler bomb about
to blow that cannot be
      defused although she shouts
at him to stop, just stop
      this nonsense now, and all
the mothers watching her
      embarrassment, appalled
but so relieved he's not
      their son, not theirs to spank
or bargain with or bribe,
      their little brat to yank
past Toys Я Us and drag
      away, while he grabs hold
of fistfuls of the greasy air
      and cannot be consoled.

PENELOPE CONSIDERS A NEW 'DO

The magazines declare don't ever cut
   your hair just after breaking up. So what
      if he's been absent nearly twenty years?
         Fact is: each day the loss feels new, the shears

still biting as the first time they'd been honed.
   Looks like he's never coming back. You've moaned
      for two decades about the shroud of bangs
         which veils your face, the way your ponytail hangs

down your back like a ragged piece of rope.
   Your follicles have given up all hope
      of *hair that moves,* of Farrah Fawcett's flip,
         Meg Ryan's shag, or anything so hip

as the pixie, the asymmetric bob.
   Go see the stylist-to-the-stars and sob
      your story out (that endless Trojan War,
         those gods). André has heard it all before.

He'll trim away dead ends so razor-fast—
   chop chop snip snip—you'll wonder why the past
      cannot be sliced so easily away
         or dyed a golden shade to hide the gray.

AFTER READING TENNYSON

Matched with an agèd wife . . .

Some gall the poet has to call
   her old. The king is just as gray
and dull to boot, slouching in
   his La-Z-Boy, a can of Coors
perspiring in his hand. He snores.
   He burps. At times, to her chagrin,
she flinches when his fingers crawl
   across the chair toward her. Foreplay
is a myth—no kisses on her ear
   or the velvet creases of her neck.
Ulysses has no fight to warm
   her now. He's blunt as a rusted spear,
but she's still sharp, hardly a wreck,
   hardly a ship lost in the storm.

ODYSSEUS, SLEEPING

Penelope barely dozed,
      while he lay still
as a coiled rope
      or a windmill
waiting for the wind
      to spin its sails. Until
he shifted in a dream,
      she sometimes feared
that he had died
      already. His beard
was tarnish on his skin.
      She often peered
beneath the sheet to watch
      his fingers twitch
with lightning storms
      in miniature, bewitched
by how his body—
      like a sudden glitch
inside the circuitry
      —was both at rest
and perching on the edge
      of action, his chest
held half between two breaths.
      Who could have guessed
that soon he would become
      a motion made
perpetual, a strange
      machine afraid
to slow, to pause, to stop
      its turning blade?

IN PENELOPE'S BEDROOM

A bottle of cologne still waits
   and waits for his return, evaporates
      to leave the passage of its scent
behind. She wonders where the fragrance went.

The right side of the bed must stay
   his side. She slips into her negligee,
      as if she's dressing still for him.
Perhaps her body cannot learn its grim

topography. She knows that life
   has dried her up. How terrible to be a wife
      made widow and yet still remain
married—what inaccessible terrain.

Whole regions that he used to kiss
   are now abandoned land. What does she miss
      the most? Without Odysseus
even her skin becomes extraneous,

a wrinkled, dusty map with few
   directions home. But long ago, trees grew
      in her, an orchard of perfume
that filled the farthest corners of the room.

WHAT ODYSSEUS REMEMBERED

Each night, they grew together near the sink,
   his shoulder kissed by hers, and hers by his,
both rinsing the day from their skins.
   First he held the soap the way a man might make
a well of his palms, bucketing the white
   smoothness there. Next he passed the Ivory to her.
He felt her hands soft and open as an orchid,
   the bar now slippery, a wet stone.
She never let it slide onto the tiles.
   Soon he bent, as if about to drink,
then straightened to watch her in the mirror's gaze.
   And then she bent the thin stem of her neck—
no words, but water beaded on her lips,
   her face the pink of petals flushed with rain.

INSTRUCTIONS FOR OTHER PENELOPES

spin what you can from his absence   a shroud
a crocheted throw in indigo and red

if mirrors crack cut jewels from the glass
comfort the muscular suitor with a kiss

comfort yourself   how long since you've been wound
or loosened from the loom   how long your hand

has worked the thread   fingered the filament
practice beauty as though it is an instrument

learn siren songs   forget the funeral hymn
pretend you are widow done with mourning

black will be the color of a tryst
and red will be a warning that you are past

the ashes of these twenty years   announce
your appetite   olives by the fistful   minced

garlic rubbed across a crust of bread
grapes giving up their stain   make an orchid

of your lips   a reckless garden of your skin
move   be still as marble   move again

call yourself mythology   converse
in rhyme in metaphor in Sapphic verse

how sweet to speak cinnamon and cloves
the taste of rosewater on your tongue   remove

your dress   the zipper opening like a V
or else imagine it   how easily

some layers are unpeeled while some remain
the pith and rind   the liquid heart   the stone

PENELOPE, PLUPERFECT

Before she had peppered
salt across her wrist,
had wrestled the heart
from its choke, had soaked
tea leaves for prophecy,
had seen a siren there,
had seen green sea, a god,
had sipped the afterward,
had tipped it down her throat,
had throttled it, had rapped
the egg to chip the shell,
had spooned the yolk from
its white bed, she licked
the liquid nova spilling gold.

PART THREE

OENOPHILIA

Those months away from you, I teach myself
to cook with wine, admiring the change
a Beaujolais enjoys inside the pot,
its sly divestment of alcohol, slowly
from the heat, like a girl unbuttoning her blouse.
I'm indiscriminate. All reds will do
because you've never had a taste for white,
the frigid chardonnay or pinot gris
so chilled it makes the crystal goblet sweat.
You're loyal to the glass of claret light.
I'm talking warmth and things that need
to breathe before they're sipped. I mean
the old varietals, picked and stomped on,
a purpled bruise delicious for its pain,
the grape skin's shredded gauze. And so I plan
a week of meals that are a lesson in
desiring, like *Tristan und Isolde,*
where consummation never comes and booze
is an excuse for letting loose again,
again the bottle spilling liquid from
its open mouth, the green neck sticky there,
our tongues discovering the metal tannins
and something close to blood, but sweeter.

ON THE EROTICS OF DEPLOYMENT

I'll build an altar
    to the tiny flecks fallen from his razor,

the pair of coveralls crumpled near the bed,
    the history of war he left unread.

The Goddess of Impermanence
    will be evicted from my home. In Her absence,

I will exhibit art
    composed of my vestigial parts,

my breasts the centerpiece
    to this display. I will be all of Greece

and Italy. I will forget about my skin
    and the awful need for friction,

how often I'm an empty plate.
    Or else, I won't forget but only tolerate

neglect. Some wives prefer
    to wait along the pier, green glitter

on their eyes, their bodies wrapped in scarlet.
    I'll try to be the harlot

that I want to be,
    Bathsheba gleaming on the balcony,

Susannah combing tangles from her hair.
      I will prepare

myself for him, a feast, a holy sacrifice.
      I'll be the fruit kept edible on ice.

SITUATIONAL AWARENESS

These past few weeks I'm more than just aware
of where he is—I'm hypersensitive,
stretched thin as a length of wire, a hair-
trigger mechanism. Nothing can live
near me. I twitch each time the telephone
rings through the dark, so like a warning bell
I want to run from it, escape the Green Zone
of this house. Who said that war is hell?
Well, waiting can be worse. Show me a guy
shipped overseas, and I'll show you a wife
who sees disaster dropping from the sky.
The ambush always comes, her husband's life
a road of booby traps and blind spots made
to hide the rock, the shell, the thrown grenade.

TENDINITIS

Stupid—the way the teacup, all at once,
weighs twenty pounds, trembling in its saucer
as though about to jump the edge, my wrist
and elbow like a pair of stunned strangers.

Turns out that living alone results in pain.
He used to haul the groceries from the car,
uncork the cabernet, screw lightbulbs in,
open the stubborn jar of marinara.

Twist, I tell my arm in the same voice
that I often said, *why don't you take
the garbage out?* How easy to dismiss
the constancy of limbs. I can barely skate

my hand into its mitten or tie my shoe.
The lesson here: lift fewer books or else
lift lighter ones. The lesson here: don't throw
a ball, don't drag a sweater from the shelf,

don't call the injury a metaphor
although it is, his absence sharp, hard
as a knob of bone, and my fingers,
clenching and unclenching what they cannot hold.

STATESIDE

If there is such
a thing as elasticity,
then we are stretched

nearly to the breaking.
The wait becomes my pulse,
come home come home.

Day eight, day nine, day ten,
day sixty-three.
When he comes home,

our miles increase,
the band pulled taut
between our separate points,

and we're released,
made slack again.
We almost don't belong

inside the same time zone,
much less this house.
He's *spouse*

instead of *lover,*
stateside instead of *overseas.*
I feel myself

withdrawing from his hand,
a touch I want
but barely understand.

VJ DAY IN TIMES SQUARE

This is how distances begin—we two,
who hurry like a pair of travelers through
our home, each room a city block,
and often we are miles from talking.
I could wave at you from a kitchen chair
as though in a cafeteria. Upstairs
becomes its own municipality.
Sometimes there is the cordiality
of namelessness, the way one passerby
might intersect then hold another's eye,
smiling before the traffic light turns green.

But opening an art book, I've seen
us in that shot by Alfred Eisenstaedt.
Remember? A sailor holds a nurse, his hat
askew so that it seems about to fall,
forever tilting on his head. She's small,
although her body curves like steel, a bridge
suspended in that kiss. There's courage
in collision. Two pedestrians touch,
embracing in a photograph with such
quick ease it's hard to know why when we meet
we're cold as strangers passing on the street.

SURFACE WARFARE

Our arguments move
across the surfaces
of things, smooth

flat areas where silence
floats for weeks.
The rule: whoever speaks

first loses. If he patrols
the living room,
then I control

our bed, an Atlantic
filled with my insomnia,
the quilts too thick

to wade through.
Some nights I think
drowning would be easier

and drink mouthfuls of salt.
No shallows here,
only the fathoms of marriage,

and we are anchored side
by side, the darkness wide,
percussive as a mine.

WINTER WALK

after Enid Shomer

The leash loops
through your fingers
down to the dog's
soft neck. I watch
you tug the strap
as though you're fishing
him out of ice.
We pause on our path,
two trees he leans
away from, and wait
for the wind to drag
winter through his fur.
The park is frozen mud,
grooved and rutted
where many separate
bodies have stood.
I think how hard
all tethers can be—
the puppy straining
to snap his harness,
or a husband inclining
into a hotter season
each time he sees
another woman
walking by. I can't
stop imagining you
turned away from me
in bed, your back
bent like a branch
when you sleep:

how easily in dreams
you could follow
the scent of something
warm, shrug me off
for the yellow slant
of sun through maples,
and then the summer
breaking from its taut
restraint of rope.

MOVING

That last night, we couldn't find our sheets
    but lay on furniture pads and barely slept,

the metal dolly in the corner of the room,
    a monster wheeled out from the gray closet

of childhood. The world was X-Acto knives
    and packing tape, boxes that spilled their secrets.

The world was a roll of bubble wrap that popped
    like a capgun going off, each wooden crate

a coffin for our valuables, a place
    to rest the porcelain vase on its side, flat

as a body. I can't say when I reached for you
    if we rustled like tissue paper, delicate

as shards, or if we slid our razored edges
    back and forth, until we split apart.

NAVY HOUSING

On Jones Street every house is painted white,
each door is white, and every yard adheres
to certain rules: the grass at crew-cut height,
an apple blossom tree bent toward the sun,
a single bush trimmed squat and round and so
symmetrically it seems man-made. No one
can deviate from others in the row.
How easily I lose myself out here.
Even the dog can barely sniff his way
back from the park. Was it a left we took?
A right? Perhaps it's safer just to stay
indoors than go off course again. Oh, look—
another flag, another garden gnome,
another sign proclaiming HOME, SWEET HOME.

BOWL, IN THE SHAPE OF
A BRISTOL BOAT

He carved the bowl for her, a hull so small
      it floated in the ocean of her palm,
rocked when she breathed, held still when she was still,

its body, purpleheart and maple,
      sanded and polished, sanded and rubbed until
the grain became a topographic map

by which to chart itself. The wooden bowl
      pushed forward, billowed a nonexistent sail.
No rudder guiding it, no mast or wheel.

The world was split between her hand and all
      the latitudes that lay beyond her hand—
a kitchen tabletop, a bookshelf filled

with Kant and Aristotle, a windowsill.
      He built the shell for her, as if to show
she was still water, and then the waterfall.

INTERSECTION

At the corner of 31st and Utah Avenue,
even the streetlights seem to watch the stag
who must be lost, six blocks from Rock Creek Park
and stranded on the numbered streets. He stands
a yard from me, posed at the edge of grass
where geometric hedges meet the curb.
Already he has chewed green furrows in
the satin robe azaleas and made
a pattern of his hooves across the ground.

I do not move. His antlers are wrought iron,
his body still like a piece of lawn furniture
left out to rust. If I were braver—the kind
who writes often about the woods, not scared
of branches stripped in winter, the smell of musk—
I would open the blossom of my hand,
hold out its emptiness. And he would taste
the drying salt or touch his nose against
my wrist, lick the vein as if it were a stream.

EASTERN SHORE

Talking about distance is a way to close
the space. Consider the bridge that curves above
the Chesapeake, which when we mention it,
becomes a child's toy. Or that the Beltway
is not a contest of families wrapped in steel,
speeding toward collision, demanding it,
but just a road that circles on itself.
Remember when we touched at twenty-two,
so willingly aligned in one twin bed,
your spine pressed up against the wall and mine
about to break over the edge? These days,
we're greedy in our king, spread wide although
we barely scrape together in our sleep.
We're isolates with only water in between.
Closeness, you used to say, closing your arms
around me like a measurement of rope.
We fell asleep to Billie Holiday,
a long, sad looping of her voice that warned
not everyone is lucky in this world.
And I remember when you dressed for work,
how I hated watching as you tied each shoe,
the tight finality of laces cinched
in bows. It's been a while since I said
the buttons on your shirt reminded me
of afternoons and evenings spent in bed,
hours now indistinct as the facing shore,
our backs like metal arches, our words moving
from mouth to caverned mouth and mouth again,
the river of our bodies murmuring.

SHABBAT PRAYER, ON THE OCCASION OF WAR

beginning with a line from Siegfried Sassoon

A flare went up; the shining whiteness spread,
      as though it were a match bright enough
to light the room, but not so bright it snuffed
        the residue of darkness overhead.
There once was darkness signifying calm—
            our candles glowed
beside the window, the nights did not explode,
      or bullets ricochet, or firebombs
turn streets to ash. We drank a glass of wine.
      The night served as the complement to day,
like salt on something sweet. And, in this way,
      we tasted syrup mixed with brine.
And, in this way, we learned a prayer
      that joined the shadow with the shining flare.